C000269789

THE
CONFIDENCE PC

By Peter English

Drawings by Phil Hailstone

"This is an excellent pocket-sized resource, packed with tips and advice for developing confidence. The scenarios and examples are a great way to bring the theory to life."
**Diane Morgan, Assistant Director of HR – Education and Development,
St George's Healthcare NHS Trust**

"Peter English has the great skill of taking complex research findings and making them clear and applicable. He respects his readers, and at the same time helps them to have the best chance they can of applying what he is teaching. This book is about building confidence and Peter is the perfect guide, taking the reader on a well-reasoned, step by step path to mastery."
**David Megginson, Emeritus Professor of Human Resource Development,
Sheffield Hallam University**

Published by:
Management Pocketbooks Ltd
Laurel House, Station Approach, Alresford, Hants SO24 9JH, U.K.
Tel: +44 (0)1962 735573   Fax: +44 (0)1962 733637
Email: sales@pocketbook.co.uk
Website: www.pocketbook.co.uk

© Peter English 2014

This edition published 2014
ISBN 978 1 906610 61 6

E-book ISBN: 978 1 908284 34 1

British Library Cataloguing-in-Publication Data – A catalogue record for this book is available
from the British Library.

Design, typesetting and graphics by **efex ltd**.   Printed in U.K.

CONTENTS

ACKNOWLEDGEMENTS

I would like to thank three teachers who have helped me to develop my thinking on the subject of confidence.

Andrew Holmes, for his inspirational work on archetypes.

David Megginson, for his commitment to the growth mindset.

Pius Hume, for showing me that confidence has to be earned.

INTRODUCTION

BUILDING YOUR CONFIDENCE

ABOUT ME

Ten thousand.

That's how many people I've worked with since 1997 when I set up my consultancy business. Part of my work is leading training courses, and it's hard to think of one course in all those years where confidence hasn't been an issue for some or all of the participants.

It's particularly apparent when the subject is how to tackle a difficult conversation, or present yourself positively at a job interview. So, the advice and tips in this book are drawn from my experience of working with all those people, hearing their stories and finding different ways to help them become more confident.

BUILDING YOUR CONFIDENCE

I'm also offering:

- Insights from everything I've read over the years – books, articles, online discussions. I take the view that my job is to sift through the research on your behalf, and then distil it down into this pocketbook

- Lessons that I've learned from my own experience – sometimes the hard way. I have been on this journey myself, so I know what it's like when you don't feel confident but want to improve

HOW THIS BOOK WILL HELP YOU

This Pocketbook is crammed with insights and practical tips. It tells you how to:

- Change the way that you think about yourself, and about your potential, so that you can start to make real progress in your life

- Move forward at your own pace, so that you are making changes without feeling overwhelmed

- Set up a multi-faceted support system that will sustain you on your journey, and help you to feel good even when you are facing setbacks

- Get a grip on the way that you talk to yourself, so that your inner critic isn't constantly undermining you

- Deal with the common confidence-shakers that we face at work

HOW TO USE THIS BOOK

There are at least three ways of reading this book:

A. Skimming through quickly, looking for advice on a particular problem that you have (for example, being nervous when making presentations).

B. Reading it carefully then, when you have reached the end, saying to yourself *'that was really interesting. I'd like to read more about this subject'*.

C. Treating the book as a practical manual, and starting to apply the tips before you've even reached the end.

For the best results, I recommend that you use the **C** approach. There's nothing wrong with looking for help with a particular problem, or with further reading, but if you only do those things you run the risk either of missing out on lots of information about how you could transform different areas of your life, or of developing a great academic understanding of confidence but not actually changing anything about yourself or your situation.

CONFIDENCE MATTERS

Confidence matters because a lack of it can stop you going after what you really want in life. It can hold you back in all sorts of ways, for example by preventing you from:

- Grasping new opportunities (a new job or promotion)
- Broadening your horizons (change or travel)
- Making an impact
- Getting things done

Confidence also matters because most people would rather deal with someone who has a confident, authoritative air. We seem to be primed by evolution to find confident people more persuasive, and to want to be associated with them. It is particularly important in situations like job interviews or presentations when you don't have much time to make an impact.

REAL CONFIDENCE

I've read a lot of personal development books over the years. Some of them have been very good but some have advocated a 'quick-fix' approach. The message of some of these quick-fix confidence books could be summarised as *believe in yourself*. I think an approach that relies solely on believing in yourself is a bit like junk food – it feels nice, can be addictive and isn't healthy in the long run.

This book is different, in that it suggests that you need to arrive at a position of **justified self-belief**. In other words, **get good at something then believe in yourself**.

So, this book will help you to develop a solid sense of self-confidence.

REAL CONFIDENCE

There are three types of confidence:

Unjustified – This is over-confidence, or confidence that isn't based on a realistic appraisal of your abilities. It is the kind of confidence exhibited on television shows like *The Apprentice* when competitors make grandiose claims about their capability and potential.

Fake – Some books, and training courses, will teach you how to *act* confidently. There is a place for this kind of advice – the chapter, Emergency Confidence, contains some tips for use in emergency situations where you are feeling anxious but need to project confidence. But relying on fake confidence can leave you feeling like a fraud.

Real – Real confidence is grounded in an accurate perception of:
- Your own abilities
- What it means to try and fail at something. In particular, do you regard failure as a catastrophe or a learning experience?

This book focuses on helping you to acquire **real confidence**.

MYTHS ABOUT CONFIDENCE

There are some commons misconceptions about confidence.

Myth

You're either a confident person or you're not

I often hear people define their ability, or their personality, in fixed terms. They say things like:

'I'm not a confident person.'
'I'm no good at interviews.'
'I can't handle confrontation.'

Reality

It's an ability that you can develop

Many people become more confident over time – sometimes just growing older can help. Anyone who puts their mind to improving their confidence will become more confident – you are not the exception to this rule! You can accelerate this process by using the various approaches described in this book.

MYTHS ABOUT CONFIDENCE

Myth

Reality

Confident people are confident in everything that they do

People who lack confidence look enviously at those who appear to be more confident and assume that those lucky individuals are confident in all areas of their lives.

Confidence is situational

You can be confident using a wide range of computer software but a nervous wreck when it comes to presentations.

Confidence is always a good thing

If you're confident, then life will be much easier. You just have to believe in yourself.

Confidence needs to be justified

Misplaced confidence can get you into trouble. For example, many new businesses fail, with one common reason being that the business owner has taken an unduly optimistic view of the business's prospects.

MYTHS ABOUT CONFIDENCE

Myth

People can tell when you're confident

I'm terrible at interviews, I get very nervous and people can always see what a state I'm in.

Reality

Other people can't see inside us

Many of my training courses offer participants the chance to practise their skills – for example in tackling a difficult conversation or conducting an interview. I notice that participants often describe themselves as feeling very nervous and confused while they practise the new skill, yet invariably this wasn't apparent to me or the other course participants.

CONFIDENCE TAKES WORK

Working life throws lots of challenges our way that can easily knock us back. You'll know that it can be hard to maintain your confidence if you've ever:

- Felt out of your depth in a new role
- Returned to work after a long absence
- Worked for a boss who bullied you
- Struggled to fit in with a team of colleagues
- Been put into a situation you're unprepared for
- Been forced out of your comfort zone

CONFIDENCE TAKES WORK

Heather

Heather had moved to London to pursue her career as a specialist nurse. Her job was very demanding and she worked long hours. Heather became miserable, not because of the work but because she struggled to fit in with the other nurses in her team. She wasn't unpopular, but when she went out with her colleagues socially she somehow felt that she didn't belong. She started to believe that there was something wrong with her – particularly in terms of her social skills. Heather had a coaching session with a consultant who helped her to see that she was in fact quite a different person from her colleagues and that she could find new friends outside work who shared her interests.

Heather was then faced with the challenge of going out and making new friends in an unfamiliar city. This would not be easy, but she felt motivated by knowing what she needed to do.

TWO KEY TASKS

If you are going to make a sustained improvement in your confidence, there are two things that you need to do:

- Undertake tasks or activities that you find challenging
- Learn to manage your mindset, particularly your beliefs about failure

The rest of this book will give you the tools you need to accomplish both of these.

How confidence works

THIS CHAPTER

Let's look first at the issue of managing your mindset. So much of confidence is about self-belief and whether or not you will allow yourself to fail, and learn from the experience. This chapter covers:

- The different kinds of mindset – 'fixed' and 'growth' – and what we mean by them
- How the mindsets apply in different contexts
- Why choosing the right one is fundamental in any attempt to develop real confidence
- How mindsets relate to situational confidence and core self-esteem

This chapter draws on the work of Carol Dweck, an American professor of psychology. I heartily recommend two of her books as a way of developing your understanding of mindsets, and how they can influence your life:

Self-Theories: Their Role in Motivation, Personality, and Development

Mindset: How You Can Fulfil Your Potential

FIXED & GROWTH MINDSETS

People with a **fixed mindset** believe that qualities such as intelligence or confidence are fixed and immutable. They say things like:

'I struggle to make an impact in meetings because I don't have strong presence.'

Individuals with a **growth mindset** have the opposite view: they believe that it is possible for you to change even quite core aspects of yourself if you are willing to work hard and explore different approaches to doing so. They say things like:

'I suspect that I'm struggling to make an impact in meetings because other people in the room are using more powerful behaviours. I need to do some research and learn how to improve my presence.'

THE FIXED MINDSET & CONFIDENCE

At the end of the previous chapter I set out the two key tasks that people need to undertake if they are to improve their confidence – ie take on more challenging tasks, and learn to manage their mindset, particularly in relation to failure. People with a fixed mindset typically shy away from a challenging task because they fear failure.

For a fixed mindset person, failure is threatening to their sense of identity and value.

People with a fixed mindset would rather maintain their image of themselves as eg, a highly intelligent expert, than risk having it challenged (in their eyes) by taking on something that would really stretch them. They interpret poor performance or failure when tackling a new challenge as a judgement on their competence, rather than something that often happens when you step outside your comfort zone.

THE FIXED MINDSET & CONFIDENCE

Druv

Druv is a junior doctor whose parents have always wanted the best for him. Since early childhood, they have praised him for his intelligence and their ambition was always that he would pursue a career in medicine. Druv learned early on that (a) intelligence is very important, and (b) he would be approved of by his parents if he demonstrated intelligence.

At school, Druv was nearly always top of the class. However, when he went on to study medicine he encountered people who appeared to be cleverer than him. One day he asked a question of a senior doctor, in front of his fellow junior doctors. The senior doctor dismissed Druv's query as 'facile' and suggested that he hadn't really understood the issue under discussion. Druv felt deeply humiliated by this encounter.

THE FIXED MINDSET & CONFIDENCE

For Druv, the senior doctor's put-down was devastating. He interpreted the doctor's comment as a judgement that he lacked intelligence. And, because of his upbringing, Druv interpreted lack of intelligence as meaning that he lacked value as a person. Badly shaken, he resolved not to ask questions in future.

In protecting his sense of value, and his perceived identity as an intelligent person, Druv has now denied himself a key way of learning and growing: he won't ask questions and debate topics as a way of developing his understanding of the subject matter. On training courses, some of his colleagues cheerfully argue with one another and with their seniors about technical subjects, whilst Druv watches in silence. If one of his colleagues loses the debate or is on the receiving end of a sharp retort from one of their seniors, they moan about it with their friends in the coffee bar afterwards but don't let it stop them from expressing their views and asking questions.

THE GROWTH MINDSET & CONFIDENCE

People with a **growth mindset** have a completely different approach when it comes to facing challenges. Typically, they say things like:

'This is going to be interesting, I've not tried this before.'

'I'm going to learn a lot from this challenge.'

'I like it when problems stretch me and I have to find new ways of solving them.'

For a growth mindset person, failure isn't threatening to their self-image – it's just some information that the tactic they tried didn't work, so they need to find another approach.

THE GROWTH MINDSET & CONFIDENCE

Mike

Mike was a hard-working junior manager who was very good at his job. But his manager called him into his office one afternoon to give him some tough feedback: *'You have a problem, Mike. I know that you're capable and that you always produce results. But I only know that because I've worked closely with you. To other people, you look anxious and as if you have the weight of the world on your shoulders. It's unsettling and it leads them to feel that they can't rely on you.'*

Mike went back to his desk feeling crestfallen. His colleague, Frances, noticed Mike's expression and asked what was wrong. Mike told her about his manager's comments. Frances helped him see that feedback is simply information about someone else's view of you at that particular moment – it's not a divine judgement. She also helped Mike to see that he could have a major influence on the way that others perceived him. After spending time with Frances, Mike identified several ways in which he could address his manager's concerns.

THE GROWTH MINDSET & CONFIDENCE

Mike invested in several books on the subjects of impact, presence and stress management. He also spent time reflecting on why he might appear worried to others, even if he wasn't feeling particularly anxious, and worked on creating a different impression.

Three years later Mike was regularly receiving compliments from other people on the air of self-assurance that he portrayed.

The key point here is that Mike adopted a growth mindset approach to his problem: with Frances' help he decided that his air of anxiety was an aspect of himself that he would work on. He then applied himself to the task of learning strategies and ways of behaving that would lead others to have a more positive view of him.

MINDSETS IN EVERYDAY LIFE

The two mindsets influence us in many areas of life. The examples in the tables on the next few pages show that the fixed mindset can hold back even apparently successful people, as their sense of value, and their identity, is often dependent on them repeatedly proving themselves. The examples we'll look at come from four common areas where people can suffer from a lack of confidence:

- Job competence
- Physical attractiveness
- Social skills and shyness
- Speaking in public

One research study found that individuals with a fixed mindset were more likely to be shy, and that shy people with a growth mindset were more likely to overcome their shyness and enjoy themselves socially.

Reference: Beer, Jennifer S. *Implicit Self-Theories of Shyness*

MINDSETS IN EVERYDAY LIFE

| Area | Job Competence |

Fixed Mindset

▶ *'I think I'm OK at my job but I would never go for promotion as I don't have the skills or the knowledge or the confidence of the people at the next level.'*

▶ *'I'm great at my job – I've been here years and I'm the go-to person in the company when anyone needs advice on logistics.'* (But I won't apply for promotion or a move even though I'm a bit bored with my job.)

Growth Mindset

▶ *'I'm going to apply for that promotion. I'm not sure that I'm completely ready for more responsibility but it will be a really interesting challenge for me, and even if I'm not successful at the interview it will give me the chance to practise my interview skills. It will also show my employer that I'm ambitious.'*

MINDSETS IN EVERYDAY LIFE

Area Physical Attractiveness

Fixed Mindset

▶ *'Unfortunately I'm not a particularly attractive person. I don't have a great body or a beautiful face.'*

▶ *'I'm naturally pretty and I've always had a good figure. I get lots of admiring glances.'* (But I won't go to that club because I've heard that there are lots of younger really attractive people there.)

Growth Mindset

▶ *'I guess I'm pretty average in terms of natural attractiveness, but I've learned how to make the best of myself by having a hairstyle that suits me, choosing flattering clothes and exercising regularly. I'm certainly not intimidated by very attractive people – I'm only interested in whether I enjoy their company or not.'*

MINDSETS IN EVERYDAY LIFE

| Area | Social Skills |

Fixed Mindset

▶ *'I'm shy and nervous when I meet strangers so I won't go to that party.'*

▶ *'I'm really confident socially, and usually the life and soul of the party – talking to strangers doesn't worry me at all.'* (But I'll find a reason not to attend Joe's birthday party because all his friends know each other really well and I won't be so high profile.)

Growth Mindset

▶ *'I've always been a bit shy but I've got better over the years. I've learned to ask people questions about their lives, and to share information about myself without dominating the conversation. I've definitely improved my social skills.'*

MINDSETS IN EVERYDAY LIFE

Area Speaking in Public

Fixed Mindset	Growth Mindset

Fixed Mindset

▶ *'I've never been comfortable talking in front of an audience. Even as a child I hated having to speak in front of the class. I blush terribly. I'm not one of life's natural performers.'*

▶ *'I'm very happy talking in front of others – I always have been. I guess I've got quite a relaxed style – I think it's easy to come across as too formal when you're presenting.'* (But I'm very attached to the idea of myself as a natural raconteur, and I don't want to admit to myself that I might need to work on my skills. So I'll continue to under-prepare my presentations and rely on 'winging it'.)

Growth Mindset

▶ *'I'm not a natural presenter, but then I'm not aiming to be one of the world's great orators. I'd like to achieve a solid level of competence, and I know that if I work hard enough at improving my skills I can be as good as anyone in my organisation. I know that I'm very aware of my blushing but I also know that other people don't notice it, so I'll try not to let it bother me.'*

HOW CONFIDENCE WORKS

CAN YOU CHANGE YOUR MINDSET?

A fixed mindset doesn't have to stay fixed. According to the research people definitely can change their mindset, and this can have a significant effect on their performance.

American researchers examined whether students who were taught how to adopt a growth mindset would perform better than those who were encouraged to have a fixed mindset. They found that the growth mindset group achieved significantly higher grades than the fixed group, with this being particularly the case for African American students.

Reference: Aronson, J., Fried, C. B., & Good, C. (2002). *Reducing the effects of stereotype threat on African American college students by shaping theories of intelligence.*

CORE SELF-ESTEEM & SITUATIONAL CONFIDENCE

If you find that you lack confidence in most areas of life, it's possible that you have a low level of **core self-esteem**.

In a nutshell, **core self-esteem** is how you feel about yourself as a person – whether, deep down, you value yourself and have a sense of yourself as being OK. The latest thinking in neuroscience combined with decades of research into child development suggests that core self-esteem is formed very early in life – probably within a baby's first six months. It seems that our early childhood experiences affect the actual structure of our brains, and the way that we develop as human beings – particularly in terms of how we feel about ourselves and other people.

Situational confidence is more superficial. It describes the level of confidence you have in different situations, rather than how you feel about yourself as a human being. So, you might be confident when networking but totally unsure of yourself when asked to write a report. Situational confidence is affected by our experiences as we go through life.

CORE SELF-ESTEEM & SITUATIONAL CONFIDENCE

MINDSETS & CORE SELF-ESTEEM

Carol Dweck examined the link between children's beliefs about whether they were able to master challenging tasks, and their ability to maintain a sense of themselves as intrinsically good. She found that children who had a sense of mastery maintained a consistent view of themselves as intrinsically good, even when they encountered setbacks. However the positive self-image of children who lacked a sense of mastery was easily undermined by setbacks. Dweck believes that this may be because the child's self-esteem is **contingent**: the message they have picked up from their parents is *we only really love and approve of you if you do well, and behave as we expect.*

References: Sue Gerhardt. *Why Love Matters: How Affection Shapes A Baby's Brain.*

Kamins, M L & Dweck, C S. *Contingent Self-Worth and its Effects on Young Children's Coping with Setbacks.*

MOVING FORWARD WITH A NEW MINDSET

The key take-away message of this chapter is:

If you want to experience real confidence in your life, you need to work on adopting a growth mindset. This might take time and effort, but it's a worthwhile endeavour – it can transform your life.

The next chapter will give you strategies to do this.

ACTION STRATEGIES

ACTION STRATEGIES

THIS CHAPTER

This chapter sets out a range of specific strategies that will help you take concrete action, and in doing so start to build your confidence. If you apply them over time your confidence will significantly increase.

The main strategies that I am recommending are:

- Setting yourself some **clear objectives**
- Using a technique called **graded exposure**, that enables you to move forward at a pace that is right for you
- Developing and maintaining your **support network**

ACTION STRATEGIES

ACT FIRST, FEEL BETTER LATER

Before introducing the first strategy, I want to clarify the importance of **feelings** when it comes to building confidence. For many of us confidence is all about feelings. We don't want to *feel* intimidated or anxious. However, a key principle of becoming more confident is that **we must not let our feelings dictate our actions**. For example, if you are in a meeting and feel shy or nervous about speaking up, it's easy to let your feelings hold you back and consequently you sit there silently and don't make any kind of impact.

The main point of this chapter, and one of the key messages of the whole book is:

Act First, Feel Better Later

In other words, if you take the right steps and face up to new challenges your feelings will eventually catch up.

Don't wait until you feel confident before you act.

ACTION STRATEGIES

USING OBJECTIVES

The first step on your mission to improve your confidence is to think carefully about your objectives. Objectives bring you focus. Three types of objectives will be useful to you in achieving your overall goal:

Type of Objective	Description
Performance	What you want to be good at and how you want to be feeling.
Learning	What you need to learn and practise if you are to achieve your performance objective.
Process	The actions you need to take if you are to achieve your learning and performance objectives.

USING OBJECTIVES

So, if you wanted to feel more confident about making presentations in public, you might set yourself the following objectives:

Type of Objective	Description
Performance	I want to be getting positive feedback from my boss on my presentation skills, and I want to feel a lot less anxious when I'm actually making a presentation.
Learning	I need to learn how to calm my nerves before and during a presentation. I also want to learn how to be a more effective presenter generally.
Process	I'm going to (a) go on a presentation skills course, (b) find out what the two most highly rated books are on the subject, then buy them, (c) talk to my colleague, Jacqui, about how she learned to be such a good presenter.

USING OBJECTIVES

SET OBJECTIVES THAT YOU CAN CONTROL

A common mistake when setting objectives is to focus on aspects that are largely out of your control.

Example
I want everyone in the meeting to be persuaded by my business case.

Although that is your overall aim, it's not helpful as an objective because it doesn't describe *your* actions. It is better to frame your objective in terms of what is largely within your control.

Example
I will make sure that my business case contains all the relevant data, and that I've circulated it well in advance to people so they have a chance to read it. I will also talk to some of the more influential members of the group before the meeting to explain my thinking and see if they have any concerns.

GRADED EXPOSURE

The second strategy that I recommend is **graded exposure**. This is an approach that is used in clinical situations such as helping people overcome phobias or chronic pain. It is also an excellent way of building confidence.

Using graded exposure enables you to gradually move out of your comfort zone but without ever being faced with an enormous and terrifying step.

How it works

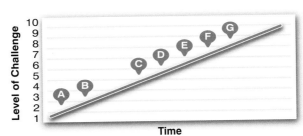

GRADED EXPOSURE

Nadine

Nadine sees herself as a shy person. She is particularly uncomfortable in large groups of people that she doesn't know well. During her annual performance review, Nadine's manager expressed the view that she needed to raise her profile and get better at networking, partly for her own career development and partly to create more customer awareness of her company's services.

The prospect of networking with strangers filled Nadine with dread.

GRADED EXPOSURE

If Nadine were to use a graded exposure approach to becoming more confident at networking, she would identify the most challenging aspect of networking that she wanted to feel confident about. This is represented by the letter **G** on the graph. She would then work backwards, identifying gradually less challenging networking-related tasks until she had identified an easy first step (**A** on the graph).

So for Nadine, **G** might mean going to a conference on her own where she knows no one, approaching ten strangers, introducing herself, telling them a little about her company, finding out about their business interests, then exchanging cards. An interim step – **C** on the graph – might be for Nadine to go to a conference but only to stay for a couple of hours and to approach three people. Step **A** could be Nadine going to a conference accompanied by a colleague, and say hello to the people sitting either side of her during the conference presentations.

GRADED EXPOSURE

GETTING THE MOST FROM THIS APPROACH

Graded exposure works really well as a way of helping you to make progress towards a daunting goal. To get the best out of this approach:

- Be disciplined – **once you have set out your plan, stick to it**

- **Take small steps often** – don't have a gap of several weeks between steps. It's important to get some momentum going or you'll feel as if you're back at the first step each time. It's a bit like going to the gym: if you're going to strengthen your confidence muscle, you need to stress it regularly. But don't go mad and try to do very challenging things every day or you'll overdo it and crash. In pain management, this is called the boom/ bust approach

- Don't take too much notice of your feelings. You will probably feel anxious, pessimistic and disappointed at various points on your journey. **The important thing is to keep moving forward**. Good feelings will come with time. To quote the title of an excellent book: feel the fear, and do it anyway. So, expect setbacks, and plan for how you will deal with them

GRADED EXPOSURE
DON'T TAKE TOO MUCH NOTICE OF YOUR FEELINGS

On the next page you can see a graph of Nadine's feelings as she works her way along her graded exposure letters. It shows that her first attempt at her graded exposure strategy didn't go well. Nadine's colleague decided at the last minute that he was too busy to go to the conference, so she bravely went on her own. However her train was delayed so she arrived twenty minutes late and entered the conference hall in full view of all the audience.

As she found a seat and sat down, Nadine quietly said 'hello' to the people on either side of her, but one scowled and the other simply ignored her. Nadine sat through the rest of the presentation wishing that she hadn't come and feeling that she would never be confident enough to interact with strangers.

It would have been easy for Nadine to give up at that point. Instead, she reflected on *why* that step didn't go well (and that it wasn't her fault), reminded herself that setbacks are normal, and resolved to try a different tactic next time – waiting until the end of the talk to say hello to the people next to her.

GRADED EXPOSURE

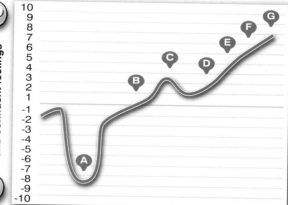

GRADED EXPOSURE
DON'T TAKE TOO MUCH NOTICE OF YOUR FEELINGS

As you can see from the graph, things got better after Nadine's first setback. At the next conference, her colleague was able to go with her and Nadine found that once she'd initiated contact with people, they seemed happy to chat.

Soon she felt confident enough to branch out on her own (point **C** on the graph) and when she hit a minor setback (point **D** was when another delegate sarcastically remarked *'You don't seem to know much about your products, do you?'* after Nadine had been unable to answer a specific question about her company's offering) she simply resolved to do a bit more research but without letting the setback affect her confidence too much.

49

ACTION STRATEGIES

SUPPORT NETWORKS

DRAINS & RADIATORS

The third action strategy for building your confidence is to **develop your support network**.

Although it's good not to need other people's approval in order to have a sense of your own worth, you'll make faster progress if you have a network of support – as long as it is of the right kind.

The narrator of Julian Fellowes' novel *Past Imperfect* describes people as being like either drains or radiators. Radiators give warmth, drains leave you feeling empty or miserable.

Try the following exercise as a way of auditing your relationships in terms of how much giving and taking is going on:

Step 1 Write your name in the middle of a piece of paper.

Step 2 In a circle around the edge of the paper, write the names of people in your life who are significant or with whom you spend a lot of time.

SUPPORT NETWORKS

DRAINS & RADIATORS

Step 3 Draw an arrow from you to each person. The thickness of the arrow represents how much you give to that person. Giving can be practical (you help them with their work, or by doing things for them) or emotional (you are supportive when they are feeling low).

Step 4 Draw an arrow from each person to you. The thickness of the arrow represents how much that person gives to you.

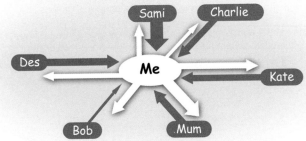

SUPPORT NETWORKS

DRAINS & RADIATORS

When you look at your diagram, what do you notice? In particular, look for whether the overall pattern is for you to be doing more of the giving. It's possible that this may indicate that your self-esteem is based on you being helpful to other people.

Relationships where you are doing much more giving than the other person aren't necessarily bad – lots of family relationships can fall into this category, but they can sometimes lead to the 'giver' feeling resentful or miserable. For relationships where you aren't happy with the balance of giving, you have a couple of options:

- Try to change the relationship. You can do this by giving less, asking for more or talking to the other person about your perception of the relationship

- End the relationship or limit your contact with that person

SUPPORT NETWORKS

YOUR SUPPORT CREW

We need different types of supporter, and different people have different things to offer. If your aim is to become more confident, it can help to have these kinds of supporters:

Practical helpers	For example, a friend with a large network might introduce you to a conference organiser who could give you the opportunity to present to a large group of people.
Emotional blankets	These are the radiators – people who help you feel better when you've hit a set-back, or encourage you when you're feeling daunted by a big challenge.
Challengers	The people who can offer you tough love, and tell you the truth when you're not living up to the standard that you have set yourself.
Peer role models	People you regard as your peers, but who are further along the road than you. It can be really helpful to know someone who used to suffer lack of confidence but has overcome it.

SUPPORT NETWORKS

HOW TO USE YOUR SUPPORT CREW

To maximise the benefit of your supporters, tell them what you are trying to achieve (ie, increase your confidence) and what sort of help you would like from them. Ask the **challengers** to kick you up the backside, let the **emotional blankets** know that you might need a bit of 'tea and sympathy' sometimes. But make it clear that you want your supporters to be honest with you on your journey of confidence development.

Consider whether any of them might want to **establish a buddy relationship** – where you provide mutual support to one another. This can work particularly well if you are both working to increase your confidence. Otherwise, spread the load around.

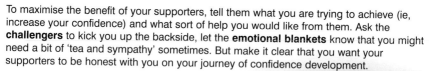

When you are faced with a challenging step, tell your supporter(s) what action you are planning to take. Psychologists have known for some time that telling people what you are going to do (public commitment) increases the likelihood of you actually taking that step.

ACTION STRATEGIES

SUPPORT NETWORKS

THE EMERGENCY PROCRASTINATION BUSTER

Here is a surprisingly powerful technique to help you overcome a challenge that you are finding particularly daunting.

Step 1 Tell one of your supporters about the action that you want to undertake but keep putting off.

Step 2 Write out a cheque for a significant sum of money (an amount that you really don't want to give away). Make the cheque payable to a charity whose work you actively disapprove of, or to your least favourite political party. Sign the cheque and date it. The date should be the deadline by which you have committed to undertake the action that you keep putting off. In this example, let's say it's the 31st of March.

Step 3 Hand the cheque to your supporter and say: *'If I don't come to you on or before the 31st March with clear evidence that I have undertaken the action that I've been putting off, then I want you to post that cheque.'*

ACTION STRATEGIES

SUPPORT NETWORKS
MIRRORS

Every day, you see in the world a reflection of your confidence levels and of how much you value yourself. For example:

- The way that your home is decorated, how clean and tidy it is, how much space there is for you
- Where you spend your time when you are not at home
- The kind of food that you choose to eat
- The television and radio programmes that you tune in to
- The clothes that you wear, how much attention you pay to your appearance
- The people that you spend time with

It's important to say that a messy, cluttered home and an unkempt personal appearance aren't *necessarily* signs of lack of confidence – but they *can* be for *some* people.

SUPPORT NETWORKS

MIRRORS

Klara

Klara used to be stuck in a job that she didn't enjoy, working for a boss who undermined her. She had no sense of career direction and was resigned to spending the rest of her working life in that dead-end role.

Klara was also a stone overweight – and unhappy about this. She spent time with several people who were drains rather than radiators, and lived in a flat that she didn't like. In her worst moments, Klara felt this was all that she deserved and that life wouldn't get any better.

Through sheer hard work, Klara gradually gained confidence and made big changes in her life. As is often the case, things started small. One evening, Klara was complaining to one of her radiator friends about how much she hated the décor in her bedroom, and the friend suggested that they make a start, there and then, on redecorating.

SUPPORT NETWORKS
MIRRORS

This gave Klara some momentum and her next task was to fix some wonky shelves in her living room. Undertaking a small piece of DIY gave her confidence a boost and over the next six months she redecorated her whole flat, revamped her wardrobe and made a concerted effort to eat more healthily.

It wasn't all plain sailing – Klara joined a gym in order to lose weight, but felt intimidated by the other gym users who all appeared confident and in-shape. Then a friend suggested that they go to a Zumba class together, which Klara loved. After 10 months Klara was feeling much happier about herself, and started looking for another job. It took five unsuccessful applications but she persevered, finally securing a role she really liked.

GIVE YOURSELF A GOOD TALKING TO

GIVE YOURSELF A GOOD TALKING TO

THIS CHAPTER

Confidence grows when you take positive action and get better at facing challenges that you previously found daunting. This chapter looks at a range of tools to help you talk to yourself in an encouraging way so that you can continue to take positive steps forward.

However, it's really important that you don't simply 'talk yourself up' (in other words, try to persuade yourself that you are doing well, when in reality you might need to improve your performance in a particular area). So two of the tactics in this chapter describe ways of seeing a situation more clearly. It covers:

- The roots of under-confidence, and why your feelings about yourself might not be an accurate guide to your real ability

- How to draw on evidence to develop an accurate picture of how well you are doing

- A technique for allocating responsibility when things go badly (very helpful if you are someone who tends to blame yourself when things go wrong)

- Self-talk: creative ways of encouraging yourself using the growth mindset approach

KEEP IT REAL

ACCURATE SELF-ASSESSMENT

If you want to be more confident, it's really important that you don't constantly undermine yourself by taking an unduly negative view of your ability and your accomplishments. Consider the case of Erika:

Erika

Erika is a lawyer. She is competent, conscientious and well respected. However, all her life Erika has been dogged by a tendency to dwell on her weaknesses and overlook her strengths. However good her work, at the end of each day she will focus on the one thing that wasn't perfect. If she did achieve perfection she would call it 'luck'.

Erika not only makes herself miserable, she can also be hard to be around. She regularly tells her friends how inept she is. When they try to persuade her that she is perfectly capable, she responds with a long diatribe presenting evidence that they are wrong. After a while her friends get fed-up with this conversational style.

Erika has a negatively-skewed perspective. She doesn't see herself clearly.

61

GIVE YOURSELF A GOOD TALKING TO

KEEP IT REAL

ACCURATE SELF-ASSESSMENT

Part of Erika's problem is that she currently has a fixed mindset approach – she doesn't believe that she is a really good lawyer. And, like Druv (the doctor whose story we looked at earlier) she is miserable because a large part of her identity and self-esteem is dependent on how well she performs professionally. However, Erika has an additional problem: her inner critic is too active.

Many of us have an over-developed inner critic who highlights our flaws and failures. We end up with an unbalanced view of ourselves and our abilities. This unduly negative view can prevent us from taking action and also cause us to feel anxious or miserable even when we are objectively performing well.

One sign of an over-developed inner critic might be in the way that you respond to praise and criticism. For example, you may have a tendency to dismiss praise (*they're only saying that to be nice, or maybe they're flattering me because they want something*) but dwell on criticism (*what did she mean when she said that I'm a nice person but I'm sometimes tactless? Am I tactless? Does everyone think that?*).

KEEP IT REAL

ACCURATE SELF-ASSESSMENT

When I work with people who have a longstanding problem with under-confidence I sometimes notice that they are very attached to their negative self-image, and in particular they don't believe that they are able to change. It's also apparent that they view their feelings about themselves and their situation as an accurate guide to the truth of the matter. So even though, as in Erika's situation, there might be lots of evidence that they are competent and capable individuals, **they let their negative feelings override the evidence**.

Why do some of us do this to ourselves? Some commentators point to cultural reasons – in the UK, for example, modesty and self-deprecation are generally seen as more socially acceptable than trumpeting one's achievements in public. Others point to the fact that imperfect parenting can leave many of us with a sense that we aren't quite good enough.

KEEP IT REAL

NEGATIVITY & EVOLUTION

Another explanation for why humans generally seem to have a bias for negative information about ourselves is offered by the discipline of evolutionary psychology.

As the name suggests, evolutionary psychology examines human behaviour from an evolutionary perspective, seeking to explain the ways that modern humans behave (and think) in terms of how those behaviours and thought patterns might have conferred a survival advantage. Psychologists who adopt this view postulate that, over tens of thousands of years, individuals who were vigilant and alert to possible danger or threat tended to survive and reproduce.

Support for this view comes from studies which show that we pay more attention to negative information than to positive, and that we are risk averse – we'd rather avoid a loss than achieve a comparable, or larger, gain.

References: Baumeister, R., Bratlavsky, E., Finkenauer, C., Vohs, K. *Bad Is Stronger Than Good.*

Peters, G and Czapinski, J. *Positive-negative asymmetry in evaluations: the distinction between affective and informational negativity effects.*

GIVE YOURSELF A GOOD TALKING TO

KEEP IT REAL
LOOK AT THE EVIDENCE

The first tactic to adopt when you want to challenge your tendency to underestimate your abilities or progress is to look carefully at the evidence. In terms of ability, ask yourself:

What is the evidence that I am competent at this task?

How much of this evidence is simply my own opinion? How much is based on feedback from others? How much is based on concrete data (for example, the amount of income that I've generated)?

After each new challenge, remind yourself to **adopt a growth mindset** and ask yourself three questions

1. What did I do well?
2. What could I do differently next time?
3. What did I learn?

GIVE YOURSELF A GOOD TALKING TO

KEEP IT REAL

THE RESPONSIBILITY CHART

The second tactic for developing a clear-sighted view of your progress is to use a responsibility chart to review what happened when you have had set-backs. The responsibility chart can be particularly helpful if you have a tendency to blame yourself when things go badly.

Exercise

Think of an occasion when something didn't go well, for example, a difficult conversation with a team member. Draw a circle and divide it into three sections according to:

- How much of the outcome was **your** fault
- How much of the outcome was **their** fault
- How much of the outcome was **the situation's** fault

GIVE YOURSELF A GOOD TALKING TO

KEEP IT REAL
THE RESPONSIBILITY CHART

Your chart might look something like this:

Their fault
- They aren't good at coping with criticism
- They are very sensitive

My fault
- I should have been more sympathetic
- I chose a bad time to do it
- I used judgemental language

The situation's fault
- We were both under pressure that morning
- Everyone is anxious because of the staff changes

KEEP IT REAL

THE RESPONSIBILITY CHART

Once you have drawn your responsibility chart, describe the difficult situation to a friend, and let them ask you questions until they fully understand the circumstances and what took place. Then ask them to draw a responsibility chart, based on what you've told them. Don't show them the chart that you have already drawn.

You might find that your friend interprets what happened in the same way that you do, or they might take the view that you have assumed too much responsibility for the negative outcome, and that you are being too hard on yourself. In which case, their chart might look like this:

GIVE YOURSELF A GOOD TALKING TO

KEEP IT REAL

THE RESPONSIBILITY CHART

Their fault
- They aren't good at coping with criticism
- They are very sensitive
- It's their job to manage their sensitivity

The situation's fault
- You were both under pressure that morning
- Everyone is anxious because of the staff changes
- These kinds of conversations are always difficult

Your fault
- You could have used more empathy, but you were appropriately firm
- You could have used slightly more tactful language
- You have the right to give your team feedback

GIVE YOURSELF A GOOD TALKING TO

KEEP IT REAL

THE RESPONSIBILITY CHART

The purpose of the responsibility chart is three-fold:

1. To help you assess the situation clearly, and identify the various factors that may have influenced the outcome.

2. To counteract any tendency you might have to assume too much (or perhaps too little) responsibility for failures.

3. To learn from each setback and identify things that you could do differently next time.

GIVE YOURSELF A GOOD TALKING TO

THE RIGHT KIND OF PRAISE

Learning to gently encourage and praise yourself is a key part of developing more confidence. It's one way of quietening down your vocal inner critic. Without this encouragement you may feel unable to move forward with the actions that you want to take. So in the rest of this chapter I've set out several powerful ways of developing a truly positive frame of mind.

As with many other aspects of improving your self-confidence, I recommend that you adopt the growth mindset when you praise yourself. In other words, it's better **not** to say fixed mindset things to yourself such as:

'I'm really good at my job.'

'I have excellent interpersonal skills.'

GIVE YOURSELF A GOOD TALKING TO

THE RIGHT KIND OF PRAISE

If you use a growth mindset approach to praise, you could say the following things to yourself:

'I'm pleased at how hard I've worked in order to master many aspects of my job. There are some areas I could still improve on, and I'll find ways of doing so.'

'I've learned a lot about how to get on with people. I think I learned some of those skills when I was a child, and I've also put in a lot of effort by going on courses and thinking about how to approach individuals. I'd like to develop my skills further by taking on more challenging leadership roles.'

Key point: With the growth mindset, you praise yourself for **effort not attainment**, and focus on what you learned rather than whether you are completely competent. Remember, a growth mindset is one of the key components of real confidence. Every time you adopt a fixed mindset you are subtly undermining your efforts to adopt a growth mindset.

GIVE YOURSELF A GOOD TALKING TO

YOUR KEY MESSAGES

As you work to develop your confidence it can be very helpful to choose your key messages – two or three phrases that you want to say to yourself as a way of giving yourself encouragement.

Examples of key messages might be:

'Everyone experiences setbacks. Learn and move on.'

'Confidence is just another skill – I can develop it with practice.'

Practice makes perfect – if I keep working at this, I will improve.'

GIVE YOURSELF A GOOD TALKING TO

YOUR KEY MESSAGES

It's best if your key messages are:

- Relatively **few in number** (so you can remember them easily)

- **Specific to you** – statements that you know you really need to be reminded about

- **Statements that you believe are true** – don't choose messages that you don't really believe. For example, some people tell themselves that *'I can achieve anything that I want'*. This is clearly not true for most of us. You risk undermining your determination to improve your confidence if you suspect in your heart of hearts that one of your key messages isn't actually true

GIVE YOURSELF A GOOD TALKING TO

YOUR KEY MESSAGES
KEEPING THE MESSAGES ALIVE

It's not enough to have identified your key messages, you need to sustain your belief in their truth. I'm not talking about the kind of doubts that might arise if some evidence appears that might legitimately challenge one of your key messages (eg, if after six months of working hard on your confidence it's apparent that you have made no progress at all). What I am referring to are those moments when you simply *feel* a bit low, and that you aren't getting anywhere.

Feelings aren't always an accurate guide to reality – you might feel low because you're tired and haven't had enough sleep, or because your blood sugar needs a boost.

GIVE YOURSELF A GOOD TALKING TO

YOUR KEY MESSAGES
KEEPING THE MESSAGES ALIVE

To help you keep your faith during the tough times, when you're feeling that you're not getting anywhere, you need to keep reminding your brain about your key messages so that they gradually become part of your habitual thinking. Remember: you may have spent many years repeating, consciously or unconsciously, unhelpful messages to yourself such as:

- *'I'm not a confident person.'*
- *'I can't really change.'*
- *'I could never do something like that.'*

For many of us, simply reminding ourselves of our key messages can be enough. However, some of us can be a little harder to convince – deep down, we don't always believe ourselves even when we tell ourselves repeatedly that something is true. If you find yourself in this situation, then I have five tips for you.

YOUR KEY MESSAGES

KEEPING THE MESSAGES ALIVE

Tip 1. Recognise that you are a sceptic. Acknowledge that you might be someone who tends to be a bit sceptical, particularly when it comes to believing positive things about yourself (you may have an over-developed inner critic).

Tip 2. Look to an external authority. See if you can find evidence from an external authority figure that supports your key messages. Sometimes we are more likely to believe something if someone else tells us it is true, particularly if we really respect that person. So, if your (possibly hard-to-please) boss tells you that you are a high performer, you might be more likely to believe their judgement than your own self-assessment. Often it's simply a case of making the effort to record and then remember the positive things that other people have said about you.

GIVE YOURSELF A GOOD TALKING TO

YOUR KEY MESSAGES

KEEPING THE MESSAGES ALIVE

Tip 3. Use auditory cues to help the message get through. So, in addition to telling yourself *'I will get better at handling this difficult situation if I keep trying'*, you could:

- Set the alarm on your phone or watch to go off at specific points during the day. When it rings, remind yourself of your key messages. This works best if you give yourself a little treat at that point – for example a cup of tea – as there is some evidence that our brains learn and remember better if the experience is pleasurable

- Put songs on your mp3 player that you find uplifting, and can associate with one of your key messages, or with your overall mission to increase your confidence. Songs can be particularly powerful as their emotional effect increases their impact

Tip 4. Set up visual reminders. For example, you might:

- Set up your computer desktop so that it displays your key messages and inspiring quotes in text form as a screen saver

- Write your messages and quotes on post-it notes that you stick to the bathroom mirror

GIVE YOURSELF A GOOD TALKING TO

YOUR KEY MESSAGES
KEEPING THE MESSAGES ALIVE

Tip 5. Use the Power Pose. This means standing or sitting in an expansive manner (ie, not hunched up with arms folded). Examples of a Power Pose include:

- Standing tall, with feet apart and arms by your sides, or with your hands on your hips

- Sitting in a chair, leaning back with your feet up on the desk

One research study found that candidates who adopted the power pose before undertaking an interview were more likely to be offered the job than those who hadn't. Importantly, the successful candidates only used the power pose *before* entering the interview room – the interviewers didn't see them in this posture. This indicates that the pose changed the candidate's internal state, and this is what made them more impressive in the interview.

Reference: Amy J. C. Cuddy, Caroline A. Wilmuth, and Dana R. Carney. *The Benefit of Power Posing Before a High-Stakes Social Evaluation*

GIVE YOURSELF A GOOD TALKING TO

YOUR KEY MESSAGES
KEEP THEM FRESH

Some of the latest scientific thinking about how the brain learns new ways of thinking suggests that **novelty** is particularly important if habitual patterns are to be replaced.

Many of the insights into this area come from the field of pain science, which helps people to overcome chronic pain. It seems that if we simply repeat the same stimulus over and over again, our brains become habituated to it, and the stimulus loses its impact. You may have noticed the phenomenon when you buy a new piece of furniture or ornament for your home, or a plant for your garden, and for a while it captures your eye. But, as time goes by, you stop noticing it.

GIVE YOURSELF A GOOD TALKING TO

YOUR KEY MESSAGES

KEEP THEM FRESH

The implication of this is that you need to keep your key messages *fresh* so that your brain still notices them. You can do this by:

- Changing the wording every so often

- Putting your visual cues (eg Post-it notes) in different places around your home (or leave one on the steering wheel of your car when you park at the end of the day so you see it next time you get into the driver's seat)

- Changing your computer desktop reminders. You may be able to set up a scrolling message, or change your desktop image to a different inspiring picture

- Ask yourself the question at the start of the day: *How many things will I notice today that will remind me of my key messages?*

As you go through the day, you might find that you are automatically alert for different sights and sounds that have an association with your key messages.

GIVE YOURSELF A GOOD TALKING TO

SUB-PERSONALITIES – YOUR INNER SUPPORT CREW

When it comes to taking on some of the big challenges in life, most people have more internal resources available to them than they realise. We turn now to your sub-personalities – the inner support crew that you can draw on to help you in your journey towards increased confidence.

'Sub-personalities' is one way of describing the different sides of yourself. However, they are more than just particular tendencies that you may have, or moods that you might experience. The idea of sub-personalities is derived partly from the work of Carl Jung, a Swiss psychiatrist from the early part of the twentieth century. Jung believed in something called archetypes: models of personality or behaviour that reside in humanity's collective unconscious and are manifested via dreams, stories and religious symbols.

The idea of sub-personalities draws on the concept of archetypes by saying that **inside each of us we have a series of different characters** that can each come to the fore at different times. These characters are often associated with the different roles that we play during our week. For example a man might be a warm, loving father, a focused manager and a respectful son all in the same day.

GIVE YOURSELF A GOOD TALKING TO

SUB-PERSONALITIES – YOUR INNER SUPPORT CREW

YOUR UNDER-USED SUB-PERSONALITIES

Your sub-personalities have particular relevance in your quest to develop more confidence because, for many people, part of what is holding them back in life is that they are **over-using some sub-personalities and under-using others**.

Michelle 1

Michelle likes to think of herself as a kind person. Since she was a little girl, she has always enjoyed caring for others, and people have warmed to her because of this. Being kind is a big part of Michelle's identity. We might call this part of her the 'kind mother' sub-personality.

When Michelle was appointed to her first team leader role, she took a 'kind mother' approach without realising what she was doing. Some of the team members really liked this – it made a pleasant change from Michelle's predecessor, who had been very focused on tasks and deadlines.

SUB-PERSONALITIES – YOUR INNER SUPPORT CREW

YOUR UNDER-USED SUB-PERSONALITIES

However a couple of the team members saw Michelle's kindly style as a weakness. They started to slacken off in their work and began arriving late in the morning. Michelle was aware that she needed to talk to the two members of staff about this, and called each of them into her office separately. She spoke gently to them about their time-keeping and productivity and explained that they should come to her if they had any problems or needed any support.

Both members of staff promised to improve. However within a few days the same problems reoccurred.

In a few pages, we'll see how the situation can have a more positive outcome if Michelle draws on some other sub-personalities.

GIVE YOURSELF A GOOD TALKING TO

SUB-PERSONALITIES – YOUR INNER SUPPORT CREW

USING DIFFERENT SUB-PERSONALITIES

Michelle's problem is one that is shared by quite a lot of new managers – how to tackle staff who consistently underperform. In Michelle's case her failure to address the problem was in part due to the fact that she was using the wrong sub-personality: ie, the kind mother, when a different personality would have been more appropriate.

For Michelle, using a different sub-personality is likely to be quite challenging. As we have seen, a lot of her identity is bound up in the kind mother, and she has little or no experience of drawing upon different sub-personalities.

SUB-PERSONALITIES – YOUR INNER SUPPORT CREW

THE RANGE OF SUB-PERSONALITIES

Some of the more common sub-personalities include:

Queen or king	**Seducer/ seductress**	**Warrior or hero**	**Grandparent**	**Child**
Acts decisively. Weighs up the facts and different perspectives, listens to other people's arguments then decides what is allowed in their 'kingdom'.	Attracts others. Is good at persuading others into a course of action by making it appear appealing.	Takes determined action. The sub-personality to draw on when something needs to be done and you are feeling lacklustre or lacking in energy.	Reminds you of what is best for you. Knows you well, and is kind. Has a sense of perspective.	Looks up to others. Innocently expects a happy outcome. Wants to be looked after.

GIVE YOURSELF A GOOD TALKING TO

SUB-PERSONALITIES – YOUR INNER SUPPORT CREW

HOW TO USE YOUR SUB-PERSONALITIES

Sub-personalities can be used in two main ways:

- To help you see a challenging situation from different perspectives
- To keep you in the right frame of mind when you are actually in the situation

The key word here is **choice**. It's best if you **choose the sub-personality that you feel is most appropriate for the situation**. Below are some examples of how you might draw on different sub-personalities.

Situation	Sub-personality
Chairing a team meeting to decide what should be done about a controversial issue that is affecting the team	King/Queen
Comforting yourself after a setback	Grandparent
Working long hours to meet a project deadline	Warrior (hero)

GIVE YOURSELF A GOOD TALKING TO

SUB-PERSONALITIES – YOUR INNER SUPPORT CREW

HOW TO USE YOUR SUB-PERSONALITIES

If we revisit Michelle's situation with her underperforming team members, here's how the story might have been different if she had been able to consciously draw on some of her sub-personalities.

Michelle 2

Michelle always likes to think of herself as a kind person. Since she was a little girl, she has always enjoyed caring for others, and people have warmed to her because of this. A few years ago Michelle realised that sometimes other people took advantage of her kindness, and that this was making her feel unhappy and resentful. She resolved to become more assertive and more discriminating about when she would show her kind side. Michelle went on some training courses and read a book about sub-personalities.

GIVE YOURSELF A GOOD TALKING TO

SUB-PERSONALITIES – YOUR INNER SUPPORT CREW

HOW TO USE YOUR SUB-PERSONALITIES

When Michelle was appointed to her first team leader role, she made a point of consciously drawing on her different sub-personalities at different points. With a young, newly-qualified team member she often used her 'kind mother' side. Within a few weeks of Michelle taking up her new post two of her team started to slacken off in their work and began arriving late in the morning. Michelle was aware that she needed to talk to them about this, but she had always found confrontation difficult and was anxious about the problem.

Michelle resolved to take some time out to plan how she was going to handle the situation. She looked at the issue from the perspective of different sub-personalities.

SUB-PERSONALITIES – YOUR INNER SUPPORT CREW

HOW TO USE YOUR SUB-PERSONALITIES

Michelle's **queen** showed her that the two staff members' performance and behaviour was unacceptable and that, as team leader, it was her role to take decisive action.

Her **warrior/ hero** resolved that she would see the challenge through to the end – she would be determined and not let the staff members continue in their underperformance. If necessary, she would use the disciplinary process.

Michelle called each of the two into her office. She explained clearly that their performance and behaviour was falling below the standard that she wanted to see in her team, and asked them directly what they planned to do about it. The staff members both looked taken aback, and somewhat unnerved by Michelle's firm approach. After the meeting there was no recurrence of the problem.

GIVE YOURSELF A GOOD TALKING TO

SUB-PERSONALITIES – YOUR INNER SUPPORT CREW

HOW TO USE YOUR SUB-PERSONALITIES

The value of sub-personalities is that:

- They give you a greater range of strategies to adopt when faced with a situation in which you lack confidence

- They provide a vivid way of bringing to life a particular approach. Rather than telling yourself 'I must make a decision', you spend some time imagining what a powerful queen would do in that situation, and bring all her clarity, sense of authority and decisiveness to bear

GIVE YOURSELF A GOOD TALKING TO

SUB-PERSONALITIES – YOUR INNER SUPPORT CREW

TRIALOGUING

Here's a second example of how sub-personalities can be used to make progress on a confidence issue, using a technique called **trialoguing**. Trialoguing is like a dialogue, except that it involves three perspectives. It can be a helpful way of exploring the different views of the parent, adult and child sub-personalities that each of us possesses.

Tip: if your parent sub-personality is sometimes stern and critical you can use a kind grandparent sub-personality instead.

Trialoguing works best if you write down the thoughts of each sub-personality as if they were in the room speaking aloud.

SUB-PERSONALITIES – YOUR INNER SUPPORT CREW

TRIALOGUING

Ben 1

Ben had always been regarded as academically capable, and had achieved a good degree at university. Unfortunately for Ben, in his first job he found himself working for a manager who was envious of him, and found ways to subtly undermine his confidence. After eight months of working in the company, Ben spotted a role that would be a development opportunity for him. He approached his boss, who immediately poured scorn on the idea, telling him that he wasn't ready for such a role, hadn't really got on top of his current job and was not the kind of person who was likely to progress quickly anyway.

Stung by his boss's reaction, Ben miserably decided that he wouldn't pursue the development opportunity.

On the next page, we'll see what happened next to Ben, and how he used the trialoguing technique to achieve a more positive outcome in a similar situation.

SUB-PERSONALITIES – YOUR INNER SUPPORT CREW

TRIALOGUING

Ben 2

A few months after this encounter Ben started applying for other jobs, and he quickly found a new position with another company. However, to his dismay, Ben quickly realised that his new manager was similar in many ways to his previous boss - ie, not interested in developing his staff, and inclined to behave as a bully towards some team members.

Ben recognised that he couldn't afford to leave this new job so soon, and decided to talk things through with his friend Sarah - who had just started a counselling course. Sarah introduced Ben to trialoguing and, a few days later, Ben tried the technique out. On the next page is an extract from what Ben wrote.

GIVE YOURSELF A GOOD TALKING TO

SUB-PERSONALITIES – YOUR INNER SUPPORT CREW

TRIALOGUING

Ben started with the sub-personality which was most apparent in what he was feeling at that time – his crestfallen child.

Child: I'm really fed up. It was hard finding another job and I was really looking forward to getting away from my awful boss. Now I seem to have ended up with the same problem. I can't keep changing jobs. I'm never going to get anywhere with my career. My parents will be ashamed of me.

Kind grandparent: Poor Ben, no wonder you are feeling down. You've not had a lot of luck with your bosses - they both sound like very difficult people to deal with. And you've always been such an enthusiastic and committed person - it must be very discouraging to work for managers who are so negative. I do feel for you. Let's just sit here for a bit and see if we can feel better.

Child: It's so unfair. I really want to do my best, and yet the people I work for always seem to take against me. I don't know what I'm doing wrong.

GIVE YOURSELF A GOOD TALKING TO

SUB-PERSONALITIES – YOUR INNER SUPPORT CREW

TRIALOGUING

Kind grandparent: I think that you've been unlucky in that both these managers are bullies. Maybe they are bit envious of a bright lad like you. What do you think?

Child: Well, maybe. I've had lots of positive feedback from colleagues and other managers in both my most recent roles.

Kind grandparent: That's interesting! Let's hear what your Adult has to say about this. . . . .

Adult: I think that what we need to do here is reflect on what these two managers have said to you, and see if there's any truth in their view. If there is some validity in your current boss's criticisms, we can address them. I think we also need to look at how you can present yourself as someone who is keen to do well, but also show that you aren't prepared to be pushed around or blocked by your manager. Let's think about how you could tackle them in a constructive way.

EMERGENCY CONFIDENCE

EMERGENCY CONFIDENCE

THIS CHAPTER

This chapter provides some tips if you need a confidence boost at short notice – eg, the day before you are due to encounter a challenging situation. It covers:

Job interviews   **Difficult conversations**   **Making presentations**   **Networking**

There are lots more tips on how to prepare for, and handle, job interviews and difficult conversations in my books *Succeeding At Interviews* and *Tackling Difficult Conversations,* also published by Management Pocketbooks.

JOB INTERVIEWS

Confidence really matters in a job interview. The recruiters want to feel that if they offered you the job you would handle it competently and confidently. However, one of the most common turn-offs for interviewers is candidates who are over-confident or 'cocky'.

Mindset

People who attend my job interview courses often say that they aren't comfortable 'selling' themselves. My response is always: *'You don't have to **sell** yourself; you just have to give the interviewers true information about yourself.'*

The problem with many candidates is that they don't give a true picture, not because they tell lies but because they don't tell the interviewers about the good work that they have done. So, the first key mindset point is: see the interview as a conversation where you give those interviewing you information about the work that you've done.

JOB INTERVIEWS

YOUR BEST SELF

It is important that you adopt your 'best self' mindset before you enter the interview room. Your 'best self' is you at your most positive. You may not be *feeling* confident but your mindset is one of *I have a lot to offer this job. I'm going to go into the interview room and give it my best shot.*

I would suggest that you spend some time thinking through your mindset before the day of the interview. Think about the key phrases that you want to say to yourself, and identify the point where you want, consciously and deliberately, to change from thinking anxious thoughts to thinking positive thoughts. This might be:

● When you walk away from your car after you've parked
● As you enter the building where the interview will be held

Once you have adopted your 'best self' mindset, keep focusing on it. **Don't worry about your feelings – expect to feel anxious**.

EMERGENCY CONFIDENCE

 JOB INTERVIEWS

PRACTICAL TIPS: FILLING YOUR BUCKET

If you want to appear confident, there are some specific actions that you can take to convey this impression. Firstly, do more preparation than you think you need to. Most candidates do the wrong kind of preparation – ie, they spend a lot of time researching the organisation that they are applying to, but not enough time thinking about what they want to say in the interview. Thorough preparation involves:

- Identifying 'what you have in your bucket'. In your imaginary bucket there should be six or seven key points about yourself that you want to get across in the interview. Aim to leave the room at the end of the interview with an empty bucket – you have left all your key points with the interviewers. Key points can be things like your skills, relevant experience and your personal qualities

- Preparing, and practising talking about, the examples you will use to illustrate the key points in your bucket

JOB INTERVIEWS

PRACTICAL TIPS: ENTERING THE ROOM

From the moment you walk in the room, the interviewers are (usually unconsciously) starting to make up their minds about you, and many interviewers rely too much on their first impressions of the candidate. These impressions are often based on things like accent, body language and mannerisms. To create a positive, confident impression, when you walk into the room you should:

- Look the interviewers in the eye
- Smile
- Shake hands

JOB INTERVIEWS
PRACTICAL TIPS: ENTERING THE ROOM

When you sit down, take up a confident posture that says to the panel (and to yourself) *I'm here to have a meeting with you because I'm interested in this job*, rather than *I'm desperate to impress you*.

A good posture is one where you lean back in your chair, with one leg crossed over the other, if that is comfortable for you.

DIFFICULT CONVERSATIONS

An air of confidence when conducting difficult conversations is important because conflict brings our more instinctual behaviours to the fore. The other person will, often unconsciously, be weighing up whether you are strong enough to see the encounter through, or whether you will back off if they put you under pressure. You need to have a confident manner that communicates *don't try and push back at me, because I am not going to back down*.

Mindset

Over the past twenty years I've met thousands of people on my training courses. Of those thousands of people, I can probably count on one hand the number that actually feel comfortable with confrontation.

So, please let go of any idea that you can expect to *feel* comfortable during a difficult conversation.

DIFFICULT CONVERSATIONS

MINDSET

The mindset that you need to adopt is:

- **Determined** – you are going to raise the issue with the other person, even if it is uncomfortable. Your king/ queen or warrior/ hero sub-personality might be the best one to have in mind

- **Clear about your legitimacy**. By this I mean that you know that you have the right to have the conversation with the other person. Your legitimacy can come from:
  - The fact that you are their manager, and it is your job to address any performance or behavioural issues
  - As a human being you expect to be treated with courtesy and respect

DIFFICULT CONVERSATIONS

PRACTICAL TIPS

One of the things that makes difficult conversations difficult is that they are unpredictable, and many of us find it hard to be confident when the outcome is unpredictable.

Gain a greater sense of control by writing down a clear objective that describes what you want to achieve from the conversation. Then think about what your next steps will be if you don't achieve your objective in the conversation, or if the other person doesn't respond in the way that you had hoped.

To reduce the unsettling sense that the conversation might become an angry confrontation, write down your key message using **clean language**. In other words, take out all the words or phrases that the other person is likely to hear as provocative. So, instead of saying:

'I'm angry at how rude you were yesterday.'

you might say:

'I'm uncomfortable with how our conversation was yesterday.'

MAKING PRESENTATIONS

MINDSET

Here are two key thoughts that can help you to feel more positive about an imminent presentation:

- **The audience are on your side**, and they have relatively low expectations. In almost every case (and you'll often know in advance if an audience is likely to be hostile) they want you to get to the point and know your topic. They don't expect you to be hugely entertaining or inspirational, so don't put yourself under that pressure

- **Your audience can't see your nerves**. Nervous presenters often worry that their anxiety is apparent to everyone in the room. The fact is that the audience can't see your heart thumping away and, unless they are very close to you, are oblivious to your red cheeks and clammy hands. And if they do get the impression that you are a little nervous, you get their sympathy

MAKING PRESENTATIONS

PRACTICAL TIPS

If you're not an experienced presenter, here are some things that you can do to boost your confidence.

- Use supporting visuals (eg Powerpoint slides) as this (a) takes the audience's gaze off you (they are looking at the slides), (b) means that you don't have to speak really well to get your message over, (c) gives you a reminder of what you want to say if you go blank

- Prepare thoroughly, and look at your subject matter from the audience's perspective. Ask yourself: *if I were them, what would I want to get out of this presentation?* This can be a confidence booster because, just by taking the audience's perspective into account, you are already some way ahead of the vast majority of presenters (who tend to focus on the topic itself and what they want to say about it, irrespective of the audience's interest)

 **NETWORKING**

Networking is a useful career development tool, and is an important part of some jobs, yet many people find it a real ordeal.

Mindset

- Don't fall into the trap of thinking that only extroverts are good networkers. **Introverts can make excellent networkers** because they tend to ask more questions of the other person. And be aware that how you *feel* about networking may not be an accurate reflection of how well you are coming across

- **Adopt a positive mindset** – an attitude of *this might be a bit awkward, but it might also be fun and interesting* is more likely to result in you having open, smiling demeanour than *I'm dreading this, and I'm sure that no one will want to talk to me*, which is likely to lead to you looking at the floor anxiously, (and make your negative thought a self-fulfilling prophecy)

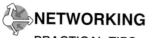

NETWORKING

PRACTICAL TIPS

- Decide that you won't stay for the whole event, or if you have to, give yourself a break. So, you might decide that at a conference you will attend two presentations, and spend 15 minutes talking to people over coffee afterwards before leaving. It's OK nowadays to give yourself a break by using your phone to check emails or go online while other people are talking to each other at an event

- Prepare some conversational openers. *'How's it going?'* works surprisingly well. It allows the other person to talk about whatever is on their mind, (eg, the difficulty finding a parking spot, or the latest piece of legislation affecting your industry)

- Prepare a way of describing your job that doesn't sound self-deprecating. If you respond to the question *'What do you do?'*, with a sentence that starts, *'Oh, nothing too important, I just.... '* it conveys to the other person that you lack confidence and/or that you are uncomfortable talking about your work

ACTION PLAN

ACTION PLAN

THIS CHAPTER

This chapter pulls together the insights, advice and tips contained in the rest of the book into an action plan. I've illustrated how each part of the action plan works by using the example of Devina.

Devina

Devina is a supervisor in a large public sector organisation, where she has worked for seven years since dropping out of university. Devina has never managed to devote much time to developing her career; she feels she has enough on her plate as a single parent with a young child. She lacks confidence at work, partly because she has gained no formal qualifications since leaving school, and partly because her various managers over the years have never shown any interest in developing her. One evening, while chatting with friends over a glass of wine, Devina was surprised to hear herself say, *'I need a new challenge.'* They nodded and agreed – *'You're capable of so much more than that job you're in now.'*

ACTION PLAN

PRACTICAL STEPS

Action	Example

Identify some specific areas you would like to feel more confident about. Commit to a maximum of three, and have only one that is *very* challenging.

For each area, conduct an honest review of your competence in this area at the moment. Try using the responsibility chart tool described on page 66. Aim to make your assessment evidence-based: look at past appraisals, remind yourself of feedback that you have received. Bear in mind any tendency to remember criticism more than praise.

Devina decided that she wanted to feel more confident about applying for more fulfilling jobs. Her aim was to move to a project management role.

Devina reviewed her skills, concluding that:
- She was very good at her job. Her productivity was higher than that of her colleagues, and she had received consistently positive appraisals for the past few years
- She needed to develop skills in project management
- She needed to feel more confident about being interviewed for jobs

ACTION PLAN

PRACTICAL STEPS

Action

Set specific objectives covering:
- Performance
- Learning
- Process

As far as possible, write objectives that are within your control.

Devise your 'graded exposure' strategy to achieving your more challenging goals.

Example

Devina set herself four objectives with a 12 month deadline:
- Develop herself to the point where she was a credible candidate for project manager roles
- Develop her understanding of project management
- Improve her interview skills
- Read three books on project management and ask permission to attend her organisation's project management training

Devina felt least confident about her interview skills. She formulated a strategy which included:
- Asking two of her friends to conduct a mock interview, and give her feedback
- Applying for some jobs that she didn't really want, just to gain the interview skills experience

ACTION PLAN

PRACTICAL STEPS

Action	Example
Think about how you will handle setbacks	Devina knew that she would feel demoralised if she was unsuccessful at one or two of her 'practice' interviews. She resolved to deal with this situation, if it arose, by: • Ensuring that she asked for feedback after the interview • Identifying what she had learned, and what she would do differently at the next interview • Reminding herself that if there is more than one other candidate the odds are against you – not succeeding isn't necessarily a comment on your ability
Map out your support network	Devina mapped out her support network (see page 50) and noticed that she was in danger of losing touch with some of her most supportive friends, and was spending a lot of time with relatives where she was the primary 'giver' in the relationship. She decided to make an active effort to spend more time with her supportive friends.

ACTION PLAN

PRACTICAL STEPS

Action

Sort out your 'mirrors'.
In the chapter on Action Strategies, we looked at the idea that our immediate environment provides us with a mirror for how we feel about ourselves.

Example

Devina felt quite comfortable with her life outside work. She took pride in her home and her appearance. However, she was aware that the clothes she wore tended to reflect her status as an administrative support worker. She noticed that in her organisation managers dressed differently from the administrative staff. Devina decided to change her work appearance so that she looked like a manager. This was partly because she wanted her organisation to see her as a potential project manager, but mainly it was a way to help her see herself in a fresh light.

ACTION PLAN

THE COMPETENCE LADDER

As we've seen, simply believing in yourself isn't enough if you are to develop real confidence. The following pages look at the steps you can take to maintain a positive mindset while you undertake practical actions to help you achieve your confidence goals.

Remember: increasing your confidence level is like learning a new skill or acquiring a habit. There are four steps that adults go through when they are learning a new skill:

- Unconsciously incompetent
- Consciously incompetent
- Consciously competent
- Unconsciously competent

THE COMPETENCE LADDER

Unconsciously Competent
Behaving confidently, and feeling confident is starting to come naturally

Consciously Competent
You are beginning to take actions that stretch you, and you're practising confident behaviours, but it feels like hard work

Consciously Incompetent
You're not very confident, and you're aware that it's a problem

Unconsciously Incompetent
You're not very confident, but you haven't admitted to yourself that you have a confidence problem

MINDSET ACTIONS
THE COMPETENCE LADDER

The two difficult steps on the ladder are **consciously incompetent** and **consciously competent**.

Being consciously incompetent is uncomfortable –
you may feel awkward or embarrassed by your lack of skill. It's easy to fall into the fixed mindset at this stage, for example by telling yourself *I'm just not a confident person*.

The other uncomfortable stage is conscious competence. At this point, there is a danger of concluding *this feels like hard work and it's not coming naturally to me. I feel fake. Maybe I'm just not a confident person*.

The way to overcome the discomfort is to **keep going**. Keep practising and sooner or later you will reach unconscious competence.

MINDSET ACTIONS

Action

Spend some time making sure that you are clear about the **growth** mindset, and how it differs from the **fixed** mindset. Identify key phrases that will help you remember to adopt the growth mindset.

Example

Devina identified two key phrases that would help her maintain a positive frame of mind: *I can do this, I'm not the first person to have moved from administration to project management and I just have to learn some new skills. It will take time, but I'll get there.*

An exercise that Devina found useful was adopting a growth mindset to review situations in the past when she had failed. She remembered that two years ago she had tentatively asked her boss if he would recommend her for promotion. He had said that he didn't think she was management material, a verdict she had taken to heart. With the benefit of hindsight, and a growth mindset, Devina saw that she could have explored his feedback, with a view to identifying what she needed to do to be perceived as ready for promotion.

ACTION PLAN

MINDSET ACTIONS

Action	Example
Resolve to adopt an encouraging attitude towards yourself. Identify the kind of self-praise that will help you grow and move forward.	Thinking about the mindsets, Devina realised that she needed to praise herself for her **effort rather than her success** (because it might take some time to achieve her main goal of securing a project management role). Phrases like *you've learned a lot from that experience, and you were brave to put yourself forward* would be more helpful than *you are a good person who deserves a good career*.
Think about your various sub-personalities – the ones that are familiar to you, and the ones that you want to develop.	Devina recognised that two sub-personalities seemed to dominate: the warrior (she never missed a deadline, even if it meant working late) and the child (she often looked for others to take the lead). Devina realised that the warrior could help her achieve her goal, but that she needed to introduce the decisive queen sub-personality, and also develop her seductress by becoming more savvy about organisational politics.

MINDSET ACTIONS

Action

Look for visual and auditory ways of keeping your key messages at the forefront of your mind, and of refreshing them so that your brain does not stop noticing them.

Write a short trialogue at the start of your confidence journey.

Example

Devina decided to put a post-it note on her bathroom mirror and set up her bedroom music system so that a song that she found inspiring would be her alarm call in the morning.

In her usual efficient manner, Devina put a reminder into her bring-forward system to prompt her to reword her key messages, and change the location of her prompts every five days.

Devina bought herself a journal that she dedicated to what she now called her *confidence project* and spent an evening exploring the different perspectives on her journey from the perspective of her child, her kind grandparent and her adult.

ACTION PLAN

TEN KEY POINTS

Now you've nearly reached the end of this book, you can be confident that you have a variety of powerful tools that will help you take great strides towards increased confidence. Here's a quick reminder of ten key points to remember as you move forward on your journey:

1. You're aiming to deliver real self-belief, not fake or unjustified confidence.

2. Confidence is something that we can all develop – it's not fixed.

3. You must take action – confidence increases when you step out of your comfort zone and face a situation that challenges you.

4. To help you move forward, set clear objectives and use a graded exposure approach that will make the challenges manageable.

ACTION PLAN

TEN KEY POINTS

5. Develop your support system – spend more time with people who are radiators, and less with people who are drains.

6. Make some changes to your environment so that it helps you to feel good about yourself.

7. Get a grip on your self-talk. Don't let your inner critic take centre stage.

8. Decide on your key confidence boosting messages then set up ways of keeping them at the forefront of your mind.

9. Remember that you have an internal support crew that you can draw on to help you face a wide variety of challenges. Use the trialoguing technique to help you keep a sense of perspective.

10. Use the emergency confidence tips when you need a boost in a particular situation.

ACTION PLAN

PASS IT ON!

Confident people are often radiators – they help others to feel good about themselves – and in doing so, the latest research suggests that they actually improve their own health.

In a large-scale study conducted in the United States, researchers discovered that individuals who were under stress but still looked for ways to help other people experienced better health and lower mortality than those who tended not to reach out to others.

So, one final tip:

> **If you want to feel better about yourself, help someone else to feel good.**

Reference: Poulin, M. J., Brown, S. L., Dillard, A. J., Smith, D. M., *Giving to Others and the Association Between Stress and Mortality*

SUGGESTED READING

If you would like to do some more reading about the ideas contained in this book, here are some suggestions for books and articles that you might find interesting.

Feel the Fear and Do It Anyway: How to Turn Your Fear and Indecision into Confidence and Action,
Susan Jeffers, Vermilion, 2007

Mindset: How You Can Fulfil Your Potential,
Carol Dweck, Robinson, 2012

Self-theories: Their Role in Motivation, Personality, and Development,
Carol Dweck, Psychology Press, 2000

Succeeding at Interviews Pocketbook,
Peter English, Management Pocketbooks, 2004

Tackling Difficult Conversations Pocketbook,
Peter English, Management Pocketbooks, 2009

Why Love Matters: How Affection Shapes a Baby's Brain,
Sue Gerhardt, Routledge, 2004

REFERENCES & FURTHER READING

Aronson, J., Fried, C. B. & Good, C. (2002) **Reducing the effects of stereotype threat on African American college students by shaping theories of intelligence**, *Journal of Experimental Social Psychology*, 38, pp. 113–125.

Baumeister, R. F., Bratslavsky, E., Finkenauer, C. & Vohs, K. (2001) **Bad is stronger than good**, *Review of General Psychology*, 5 (4), pp. 323–370

Beer, Jennifer S. (2002) **Implicit self-theories of shyness**, *Journal of Personality and Social Psychology*, 83 (4), pp. 1009–1024

Cuddy, A. J. C., Wilmuth, C. A. & Carney, D. R. (2012) **The benefit of power posing before a high-stakes social evaluation**. *Harvard Business School Working Paper*, No. 13–027

Kamins, M. L. & Dweck, C. S. **Contingent self-worth and its effects on young children's coping with setbacks**. Unpublished data, cited in *Self theories: their role in motivation, personality and development*, Carol S. Dweck. Psychology Press. 2000.

Peters, G. & Czapinski, J. (1990) **Positive-negative asymmetry in evaluations: the distinction between affective and informational negativity effects**, Stroebe, W. & Hewstone, M. (eds.), *European Review of Social Psychology: Volume 1*

Poulin, M. J., Brown, S. L., Dillard, A. J., Smith, D. M. **Giving to others and the association between stress and mortality**, *Am J Public Health*. 2013 Sep;103 (9):1649-55.

About the Author

Peter English

Peter has twenty years' experience of helping people
to achieve their potential and get the most out of
their working lives. Since 1997 he has run his own
consultancy practice and during this time he has
coached and trained thousands of people in how
to be more effective in their dealings with others.

Contact

Peter can be contacted via his website www.peterenglish.co.uk.